ENDORSEMENTS

I enjoyed this book immensely. It boosted my faith. The testimonials were clear and excellently written. Prayers and Scripture suggestions at the close of the book were spot on. I *really* enjoyed reading Supernatural Encounters with God: The Catalyst for Healing.

Dr. Santos Rivera, MD
New York, USA

We loved this easy to read, inspirational record of God's healing work. It is not a religious, one-size-fits all account. It really is a series of testimonies about how a relationship with the Holy Spirit led to miracles. Get ready to get into the healing move of God. At times we were filled with awe. At times we were filled with wonder. At times we were filled with strength. At times we were filled with joy.

All that to say, faith came to an all-time high! Nothing is too difficult for our God. These supernatural encounters were so riveting that neither of us could stop until the last page was experienced! MK's writing is refreshing, believable, doable and current with the present truth of the love and power of the Holy Spirit.

Pastors Sandy Newman and DeeAnn Ward
Destiny Ministries
Arkansas City, Kansas

Supernatural Encounters with God: The Catalyst for Healing – 25 True Personal Stories of Activating God's Healing Power, is a riveting book by MK Henderson that offers a myriad of ways, including nine powerful prayers, to achieve optimal health. Throughout the 25 chapters, we receive expert and spiritual solutions to today's health issues that impact millions around the globe. Easy to read and understand, this book uplifts the hopes of its readers while offering practical tips that can be implemented toward a speedy recovery. A great read! Bless you, my friend!

Rev. Kevin Wayne Johnson
Founder and CEO,
Writing for the Lord Ministries
Clarksville, MD (USA)
Author – *Give God the Glory!* series
www.kevinwaynejohnson.com

God has said we are to pray "His will be done on earth as it is in heaven," His rule and reign, His Kingdom established right here on earth. There is no sickness nor disease in heaven. MK's life has been one of believing faith and taking God at His Word. Years of experience, listening and seeing God move in miraculous ways will challenge and encourage you to press into Him and grow in your faith as you read Supernatural Encounters with God: The Catalyst for Healing.

Pastors Steven and Meredith Giles
Mt. Moriah Church and Ministries
Glenmont, NY

Supernatural Encounters

with

God

The Catalyst for Healing—

25 True Personal Stories of Activating God's Healing Power

by

M.K. Henderson

Supernatural Encounters with God
The Catalyst for Healing–25 True Personal Stories
of Activating God's Healing Power

Copyright © 2020 By MK Henderson
Brand New Images, Inc.

ISBN- 978-1-892-555-090

Scripture taken from the New King James Version®. Copyright © 1982 by Thomas Nelson. Used by permission. All rights reserved.

Disclaimer: This book is for informational purposes only. While every precaution has been taken in the preparation of the book, neither the author nor the publisher shall have any liability to any person or entity with respect to any loss or damage caused or alleged to be caused directly or indirectly by the information contained in this book. Most names and identifying details have been changed to protect the privacy of individuals involved.

Printed in the United States of America

DEDICATION

I dedicate this book to my mother, MA Henderson, who has diligently taught me the Word of God from childhood. Her belief in angels, healings, and miracles caused her to say, "God can do anything because nothing is too hard for him."

My mother lived life according to her beliefs. She was healed of high blood pressure she had since her forties. Her doctor was surprised and asked what treatment cured it. Now, with normal pressure, she would never need surgery for heart valve prolapse. She boldly informed him that God had healed her.

I am also dedicating this book to those suffering who don't see a way out for optimal health. I am *not* offering medical advice. I am only telling my stories of healing miracles. I am not a medical doctor, but I know the Great Physician, JESUS (Yeshua) Christ. God doesn't cause sickness in his own children. He hates it. I pray this book imparts hope and faith to you.

CONTENTS

FOREWORD

The Church of the 21st Century does not have the boldness, by and large, to move out in faith to ask for the healing of our physical bodies, simply because they have not been apprenticed in the way of doing it. This type of ministry matures as a person witnesses seeing an individual actually pray in an effective way over a grave physical problem and the positive outcome. In the healing summary, MK tells you how to step out in faith and how to pray, believing God for healing.

You will notice that MK doesn't completely discount the medical profession, but puts faith to work on a diagnosis receiving proof of efficacy when a miracle happens. This is an excellent model. To make use of God's provision of nutritional substances also makes good sense.

To pray for healing seems like the way to go in **all** cases so we can accurately target our prayers following a diagnosis. Doctors can only do so much, so our faith has to be completely in God, our Creator. When the doctor says we have been healed without the need of surgical intervention, a major victory has been achieved, and God receives all of the glory!

~Doris Wagner, Minister
Glory of Zion Intl.

INTRODUCTION

In this book I am displaying some of the diverse healings that my family and I have experienced. I hope these stories will encourage your heart to pray for your family. I pray that as you read of the miracles in this book, you will be inspired to step forward boldly in faith—ask for God's touch, believe he desires to heal you, and trust in his promises. Pray and keep on praying. Be reassured that whatever you are going through, Jesus is with you. He loves you and will see you through your fiery trial. If you desire to read about worldwide miracles and healings, most of which I personally witnessed, you should read my book *Supernatural Stories of Hope and Healing: True Inspirational Reports from Around the World.*

I met Jesus at the tender age of eight years old. He has remained a part of my life through my college years and graduate school and in fulfilling various jobs. I'm always learning more about Jesus and getting to know him experientially, so my relationship with him gets deeper each year. As I face new challenges, he is with me and his fierce love is fighting for me to be an overcomer.

The Bible says we overcome the destroyer by the word of our testimony and loving not our lives unto death. The book of Ecclesiastics says the day of death should be a cause for a celebration more than the day of birth!

I learned that God heals in various ways. The heavenly Father has made a way for our optimum health, and Jesus took the whip tearing into his flesh so that we may be healed (Isa. 53:5 and I Peter 2:24).

The Holy Spirit heals our bodies by releasing his power. The Holy Spirit is here on the earth; he speaks to us in our spirits, instructing us how to live in divine health to remain healthy. Our body is like a vehicle. If oil changes and tune-ups are done regularly, the vehicle will run well and last many years. But if not maintained, it will fail you. Do we take better care of our vehicles than our bodies? One may acquire another vehicle but not another body on this earth, at least not legally and ethically.

As a child growing up in the Midwest, I saw wheat and cornfields as far as I could see. Most people lived a simple life. Not much has changed to this day. You plant, water, and harvest; that's it. It's a simple life without a lot of money, but enough to meet one's basic needs. A few big farmers lived in the area, and my dad was fortunate to work for one of them, a kindhearted man. The area was considered a depressed one, rating as next to the poorest county in the region.

My mother's family was one with a strong faith in God. Her father was a hard farm worker and entrepreneur, and although he faced many challenges, he always seemed to overcome the worst of them by his faith in God. Father of ten children, living on a farm with the nearest neighbor miles away, many times he had to be creative and inventive. My grandfather didn't depend on others to meet his needs or even help much. He was strict with his children, regularly having family devotions and requiring all of them to be in church on the Sabbath.

When my grandmother suffered a stroke, he didn't believe her condition would be reversed by taking her to a doctor, especially in those days when there wasn't a remedy for strokes. She eventually died when my mother was fifteen.

My mother was his youngest daughter, but was far from being babied. At the age of nine, she had her assigned responsibilities, taking care of the family's wealth, turkeys. She was their caretaker on the prairie and killed rattlesnakes and other threatening creatures that came near them. The biblical David had sheep and she had turkeys. That is probably where she learned to become a prayer warrior! Another thing, children were not allowed to be sick in that home. Many days she walked several miles to the country schoolhouse with colds and flu in blizzard conditions, half frozen when she arrived.

My mother only had a fifth-grade education, but one would never know it as she competently managed the books and did the budgeting in our household. Like most families we had just enough to make ends meet, and that did not include medical bills. So rejoice, laugh and cry with me over the miraculous healings our family experienced throughout the years.

This book is Volume 1 with accounts of twenty-five healings. Volume 2, *Creating a Supernatural Lifestyle,* is coming soon, also with twenty-five accounts of angelic encounters and miraculous answers to prayer.

PERSONAL HEALINGS

1

HAY FEVER AND ALLERGIES

While most people were eager for the warm weather spring would bring, along with the blooming of perennials, blades of grass shooting up and birds singing their melodies, I dreaded spring as it was the onset of my hay fever and allergy symptoms, also blooming. When I was around eight or nine years old I developed severe hay fever and allergies from being out in the fields occasionally. At the time I didn't realize the primary allergen was probably dust.

I was miserable five months a year, but it was something I would have to live with since we didn't have extra money for doctor visits. However, I visited the clinic once and was diagnosed with enlarged tonsils. A tonsillectomy was recommended, along with over the counter meds which didn't cure me of the allergies or even take away the hay fever symptoms for very long. They usually made me sleepy and drowsy and unable to concentrate.

My mother had prayed for me many times, but it appeared that her prayers just weren't getting through! I woke up early at 6:00 a.m. most mornings sneezing non-stop about thirty times, with eyes nearly swollen shut and nose running. A low-grade fever was also the norm since spring had arrived. It seemed the older I grew, the worse the symptoms. My mother felt bad for me and said, "Looks like you are worsening day by day. I wish we could find something to help you!"

Cleaning the natural glue out of my eyes so I could fully open them and blowing my nose each morning became a daily routine. I would sit in school all day just miserable and hated gym class as it seemed to aggravate the symptoms.

Finally, school was out for the summer. Yeah! Now I could at least stay home and remain indoors, which decreased the symptoms a little. At the same time, my brothers and I were expected to ride to the fields with our parents to help pick corn and whatever else was growing out there. Working in the fields only fired up my hay fever and allergy symptoms.

I prayed, "God, please heal me or show me a solution!"

A few years later as a teenager, I would spend at least an hour a day in the afternoons at the local library less than a half mile from my home. Due to air conditioning in the library, my symptoms would decrease a little. I loved to read and was especially drawn to Nancy Drew mysteries.

One summer I had a brilliant idea, why not research a cure for my misery? I would be a senior the next year, and I dreaded the thought of going away to attend college in my condition. I began looking for books about hay fever and allergies. I ended my research with hope that a change of diet would cure it. My diet was a typical teenager diet with lots of carbs, etc.

I decided to begin with an all juice diet and took on a part-time job helping to reorganize the school library a couple of hours a week. I used most of that money to buy extra fruit and juice that summer. After three weeks I noticed a remarkable improvement! My symptoms had lessened substantially. I continued that routine and by the time I was ready for college, I had very little symptoms at all. God healed me by showing me what I needed to eliminate from my diet and what to take in to restore balance. Of course, I didn't know at that time I was actually detoxing my body. Sometime later the doctor also discovered my tonsils had shrunken and a tonsillectomy wouldn't be necessary.

2

GYMNASTICS CLASS GOES AWRY

It was my freshman year of high school and I was excited and a little intimidated at all the new faces. My most hated class was gym, but there was no way of getting around it as it was required, and for good reason. My school was one of the best in the area in sports. The students worked hard, played hard, and took the victories!

Today I was taking my first and last gymnastics class as a part of the PE requirements. The teacher was a young man and eager for all the students to participate in the gymnastics routine. In the rural areas, teachers taught subjects that they knew nothing about. This was clearly the case here. Although this teacher was well liked, he didn't have much knowledge of gymnastics.

One day we were doing routines on the mat in girl's gym class, and these routines required great flexibility in one's back. My back was not flexible, but the teacher insisted that I keep trying the routine. Each time the routine was completed incompletely, I experience more pain in my back. Finally it snapped and I could barely raise up off the mat to stand.

The class ended abruptly. I was in great pain. Someone assisted me as I stood and limped to the locker room. My friend Britney helped me dress and cross the street to the medical clinic. At this small clinic there weren't any X-ray technicians, so the doctor took his own X-rays. There was a lot of scurrying around and whispers between him and his nurse, who was also his wife.

Finally, the doctor informed me that I had a serious back injury. I would not be able to walk home, which I already knew due to the extreme pain I was experiencing. He instructed me to remain on bedrest for several weeks without doing any housework and warned me that if I did try to do any work I would surely risk becoming paralyzed for life.

When my mother came and picked me up, the doctor was unavailable so no one at the clinic gave her a diagnosis about my condition. A couple of weeks later, the clinic called our home and informed us that they had ordered a large back brace for me to wear and that my mother should go to the clinic as soon as possible to retrieve it, as I would need to wear it at all times.

The next several months I experienced the worst pain I had ever had in my life. I was bedfast and spent the days moaning and listening to the radio. My mother had a program which she loved to listen to each morning. On her favorite program they talked about people sharing the good news with people in distant lands. I was especially interested in Mexico, so when that country became the topic of the day, I ordered the books that were offered to read up on the country.

When the package arrived I spent quality time praying and focusing on Mexico instead of the chronic pain that nothing seemed to decrease. There wasn't any medication strong enough to ease the pain. Taking aspirins was like eating candy. My mother and I prayed daily for healing for my back. My new pastor and his wife also prayed often for me, sometimes coming to the home to pray since I couldn't attend church services. The huge back brace that I was forced to wear only caused the pain to increase. After a year of this I realized I would have to live with the pain and try to manage it until God healed me.

I returned to school clinging to the staircase as I went from class to class. I only had a couple of friends attending that school. They were not in my class so they were of little help to me. My parents or the school system didn't consider home schooling. It was unheard of in that area. I managed to complete the school year with decent grades.

My pastor and his wife continued to pray for me and believe God for my complete healing. Over time, gradually the pain decreased, and I could function a little better most of the time. Then one day the pain all disappeared, but I had to be extra careful not to stress or strain my back as it wasn't strong yet. I thanked God for my healing.

The injury being in the lower back, I was left with one leg shorter than the other, so I walked with a slight limp. One day, while in a worship meeting, I was thanking God for his goodness and a guest speaker, whom I had never met, asked me to come to the front of the sanctuary to receive prayer. I obeyed him, wondering what he was going to pray about. Immediately he began to ask me about my back and legs. He stated that due to a back injury, one of my legs was shorter than the other. I had become so accustomed to walking with a limp that I didn't worry about it but just accepted it.

He prayed for me and as I was walking back to my seat it felt as if I had put on a new shoe, one with a lift inside of it, as both legs were now the same length. A miracle had taken place as my pelvic area had straightened out allowing me to walk evenly.

Many years later I finally discovered the extent of the injury. I began having pain in my neck and upper back versus the lower back where my gymnastics injury had been located. I contacted a chiropractor and made an appointment. He examined me and inquired if I had any previous back injuries. I explained about the gymnastics injury. He asked to see the X-rays. I informed him that he would need to order them if he really needed them.

He said, "I wouldn't even think of touching your neck or back without seeing those X-rays first."

I gave him the address of the doctor and signed the release. I didn't think the files could even be located since the previous doctor had retired and left the area many years prior.

A couple of weeks later the chiropractor called me to come into his office. Upon entering he asked, "Why didn't you tell me you had fractured several vertebrae in your back?"

I was shocked. "I didn't know I had a broken back!"

He said, "Look at these X-rays."

He pointed out all three fractures in my lower back.

I said, "I am shocked! My family and I weren't informed by the doctor about any fractures."

The doctor was probably working with the school to insure there wouldn't be any liability.

The chiropractor said, "One thing I don't understand. How did your fractured back heal?

I told him the doctor didn't recommend any treatments, other than to wear a heavy back brace which increased my pain. It became unbearable so I finally just quit wearing it. The chiropractor surmised that the brace would have likely pulled the vertebrae further apart!

My God is a God of the impossible, and he completely restored my back.

3

LOCKED IN A BOX

I entered the classroom and took a seat in the back of the room, as far back as I could go without actually touching the wall. I was in reading class and hoping to just be invisible to everyone. All through elementary school and most of high school I was what some people called "Locked in a Box." I had such a high level of fear and anxiety that I rarely spoke outside my home.

One by one students began to read as the teacher, Mrs. Johanson, began calling names of students to read. She called my name and I froze. She repeated the request and I opened my mouth, but not a sound came out.

With time, I started to read a few words, then another, and that was about it. I couldn't go any further. By now the teacher was accustomed to my non-performance in this area and went on to the next student.

I loved going to church with my family. We usually attended services two or three times a week. We would go Sunday morning, Sunday night, and Wednesday night. It was a small country church. Our new pastor had a very unusual story. He was also very strict with us teenagers. After hearing his story we could understand why he was such a serious man, although he showed a little sense of humor at times.

This pastor had been working as a mechanic and was under a truck when the lift shifted and the truck came crashing down upon him, crushing his body. His eyes were pressed out of the sockets. and of course, blood flowed everywhere. He recalled seeing a great light. He knew that Jesus was with him.

Upon arrival at the hospital in the community where he was living, he was declared as good as dead. But his wife would have none of that; she prayed, believing God would restore her husband. Yes! God did it and she got her husband back.

To look at this pastor, one would never know he had endured so much suffering and had received a huge miracle. He and his wife were compassionate and concerned about our spiritual well-being and became involved with our family.

One day the pastors spoke to me about leading the youth group. I declined as I could not speak in public. They tried another angle. They said that God had a plan and a purpose for my life that involved speaking. I cringed at that idea and withdrew. However, I did pray about it in my quiet time with God in the evenings.

I guess I was hoping to hear a booming voice out of heaven saying, " NO! You do not have to speak before people ever! That is definitely not a part of my plan for your life."

But no . . . that did not happen.

One Sunday the pastor and his wife approached me, telling me they were going on vacation and wanted me to put together a message and fill in for them. *Oh no*, I thought. *Here we go again!*

I panicked, thinking I could never do that. I replied, saying I would have to pray about it. I had a few weeks before they were to leave, so I hoped they would just forget their request of me and seek out another.

In the meantime, we had a very unusual service one Sunday night. The power of God was flowing as we worshipped, singing the usual choruses and hymns. People began to cry; some were shaking as others were speaking in an unknown language, seemingly without effort. I felt God's love being poured out upon me in a huge way. As I closed my eyes and worshipped, I saw a vision of myself speaking before a large crowd of people in Mexico. At that moment it seemed the Lord loosed my tongue and I began to speak and worship in an unknown language, a heavenly language. It was exhilarating!

This phenomenon is recorded in Acts 2:1-21. It is praying in tongues with your spirit. Research done in the UK on 1,000 people concluded that those who experienced this regularly have fewer mental disorders than those who do not.[1]

A couple of weeks after that experience I realized something had happened within me. I had experienced inner healing and could now read out loud in classes and did not feel the constriction on my chest at the very thought of speaking in front of people. God had done something deep inside of me, a type of inner healing. I no longer felt intimidated at school and even shared my experience with a few people. So when the pastors approached me, again requesting I prepare a message and give it while they were on vacation, I acquiesced, and informed them I would give the message.

Soon my big day came, and we had many visitors. It seemed that people came from other places to hear me, but they didn't even know I was speaking, nor did they know the pastors were to be on vacation that Sunday. Of course, I thought perhaps they had heard and came to see the circus. I gave the message with knocking knees, and the visitors came around after the service, complimenting me on my first sermon.

My senior year in high school, I became acquainted with the speech teacher whom most students affectionately called "Mrs. J." She was a sixty something short stocky woman who sported a gray and black bob. Mrs. "J" was very committed to teaching her craft.

She must have heard about my inability to speak before a group because she approached me one day with the offer of a part-time summer job working with her in the high school library. There really wasn't much work for me to do on that part-time job, and she didn't come in daily to supervise me. At the end of the summer, she asked me if I would be taking her speech class when school began.

I was speechless as we had become pretty good friends during the summer. I didn't know how to respond. At first, she was very low key about it and said it would be a good experience for me.

I told her, "I can't speak well in front of groups."

She said, "Nonsense, you will do fine and have fun and enjoy the class."

Maybe, I thought to myself. Well, one didn't mess with Mrs. J, so I reluctantly consented. After all, she did go out of her way to single me out for that part-time job.

Our first assignment in Mrs. J's class was to write a speech on democracy. There were only five or six people in her class. I think she handpicked them all, as most were like me, inept at speaking before a group. I worked very hard on my democracy speech. She later informed us that we were going to be giving our speeches not only in class but also on television. Sure enough, after we practiced our speeches in class, we were entered in a contest without our prior knowledge!

We drove to a nearby community to the CBS television station and delivered our speeches the best we knew how. Apparently, we were a hit and were asked to return. One thing led to another and the next thing I knew, Mrs. "J" as recommending me for a communications scholarship at a college!

The coming fall, I enrolled in a private liberal arts college with a communications scholarship which included an emphasis on drama. While in graduate school I became the co-anchor for a national news program. The rest, as they say, is history.

4

New Jawbone

Having just completed my master's degree, I was excited to be moving to New York City for a new job. I visited my brother in the Midwest and while there, had a dental checkup. I was experiencing pain in the upper right jaw. As a student, I hadn't always received my checkups on schedule. I experienced a very negative situation with a dentist, while in graduate school, so I wasn't eager to have future appointments.

My brother explained that his dentist was very efficient, compassionate, and competent. I actually looked forward to the appointment he arranged for me.

Dr. Brock was very friendly and no nonsense. He examined me and explained the source of my pain. I had an impacted tooth that had triggered an infection under the gums and in the bone. He informed me the only cure was to cut the gums, peel back a portion to expose the infected area of the jaw, and scrape the bone to remove the infection.

"This will really be a major surgery," he explained. "However, the recovery time will be short."

I decided to think about it as I didn't want to begin a new job in a new city immediately following surgery. I prayed about it and decided to follow up with a dentist after getting settled in New York City. I also needed a good dental insurance policy before I opted for this procedure. I decided to wait until I had been working at least a month and then make an appointment.

A few months later I had an appointment for a cleaning, exam, and X-rays. I did not mention the problem with my jaw as I knew if it still existed it would be seen on the full mouth X-rays. The dentist returned to me with all the films and said something I will never forget.

He said, "I see you had a jaw problem at one time, but now it appears that it's okay. The problem has been eliminated."

I asked, "Do I have any infection?"

"No," he said. "Look at this X-ray! You have grown new bone in your upper right jaw!"

5

MYSTERY SOLVED

Fast-forward twenty years and I am at the university medical center in Denver. I am getting a checkup but also complaining of pain in my *lower* right jaw. The previous problem was in my upper *right* jaw. They took many X-rays and then consulted about a strange phenomenon they were seeing.

Earlier, another dentist in a private practice had informed me that I would need dental surgery on that lower right jawbone, but she didn't really have a name for it. She added that I would need to see a dental surgeon, to cut out a large area of my jaw to keep infection from spreading. I visited a dental surgeon, but of course they had nothing else to offer besides surgery.

Now the university medical center was going to get to the bottom of it. The specialists decided there was a name for this rare condition. They informed me it is usually seen in Native Americans. They gave me two options. The first option was surgery; the other was a hyperbaric chamber. I googled the diagnosis to check my options online. There weren't many. I studied the surgical outcomes and realized most patients who had the surgery didn't improve or the problem returned after surgery.

I couldn't locate even one clinic or hospital with a hyperbaric oxygen chamber in the area. I left the dental office, and the next day was visiting with my chiropractor about some nutrition products. He mentioned that he had a new machine that acted like a hyperbaric oxygen chamber to the tissues in the body. I informed him of my problem. He said I was welcome to try it although he couldn't guarantee it would work for my problem.

I went several times a week for a couple of weeks and realized there was no more pain and infection. I believe God directed me there. The chiropractor *just happened* to have the new machine that everyone was trying out for soft tissue injuries after accidents. He *just happened* to mention it to me and gave me some materials about the machine. I read the materials and realized it was the type of hyperbaric oxygen machine I needed.

6

NEW SHOULDER

Some people have written about dying and going to heaven and while there seeing body parts for people. My first thought was how weird that seemed, but after a couple of shoulder injuries I am beginning to become a believer.

I was working in NYC as a media relations director for a large international, non-profit organization. I left my home at 7:30 a.m. and traveled by subway an hour to lower Manhattan. Then I walked a few blocks to my office. This was a very busy time of the day; taxis, automobiles, trucks, and even messenger bikes rushed to get to their destinations first thing in the morning.

This particular morning I was about a block or two from my office and had just stepped off the curb to cross the street as traffic was stopped. But as I took my first step, I was practically knocked down by a messenger bike. My shoulder was hit at an angle such that it partially dislocated. A hospital was just down the street, so the police suggested I go directly there. At the hospital they took X-rays and examined me. Thankfully, there were no broken bones, but I had a very bad sprain to my rotator cuff. I was given pain medication and a sling and released.

Although I wore the sling, the pain did not decrease at all. Rather, it increased each day. Of course, doctors always wanted to talk about surgery, but I was not considering that. I knew others who had rotator cuff surgeries. Some of them had favorable outcomes and others were still suffering. So I stood in prayer lines and believed God for healing.

After a few months I noticed a slight improvement. My shoulder regained strength and improved until I was completely healed. So much so that I was able to work out and do aerobics at the gym!

7

OUT OF CONTROL TREADMILL

Many years later, I was thrown from a malfunctioning treadmill at a community center. My shoulder blade and rotator cuff were seriously injured. All the physical therapists, chiropractors, and doctors suggested surgery. Yet, I did not want to consider that. Since I had heard people had seen replacement body parts in heaven, I decided I'd request a new shoulder.

The medical people all advised that this was a serious injury, and if it even healed, it would take at least a year or longer.

Several friends encouraged me to continue praying about it. I saw a massage therapist, but that didn't seem to help much. After six months, I began doing a little physical therapy on my own a few days a week and continued for several months. One of the doctors recommended a natural pain killer, medication to manage the pain since I wasn't scheduling surgery.

I realized one morning that I could actually raise my arm above my head. I had been unable to do that for nine months. God had given me a new shoulder. I could do anything I wanted to do!

8

WINE OR WATER

ine is mentioned many times in the Bible, and Jesus turned water into wine. I often wondered if the well water people drank in those days was mostly impure and caused illnesses. The apostle Paul advised Timothy to take some wine for his stomach (1 Tim. 5:23). Jesus turned the water into wine at a wedding. Could it be that Timothy and others frequently drank impure water and needed the wine to kill off the bad bacteria upsetting the stomach? They didn't have water purifiers like we use today when living in third world countries.

Most people living in developed countries such as the UK and USA, take clean water for granted. Although I have lived in third world countries, I had no idea of the severity of the damage that can take place in a person's body from unclean drinking water until experiencing it firsthand.

When I relocated to New York City right after graduate school, a pastor friend arranged for me to rent an old house from some people he knew in a Bronx neighborhood, near the West Chester County line north of Manhattan. The house was really a dump! I guess he thought I could handle it until I found a more suitable place. Most of the people in the neighborhood were from the Caribbean Islands. The pastor also informed me it was a very safe neighborhood, as people here believed in an "eye for an eye" in this area. The area was mostly crime free due to the strict neighborhood watch and the way they dealt with crime.

I am basically a healthy person, but shortly after I moved into the house and began working at my new job I exhibited frequent infections in my respiratory, urinary, and digestive systems. This went on for a few months. Finally, after seeing a doctor, I decided to check the water as the pipes were very old and rusty. I took water samples to a lab and had them analyzed. The report arrived in the mail, and guess what? Bingo. This water was full of e-coli bacteria and other deadly organisms. This water was worse than the water in some third world countries!

I began seeing a famous natural medicine doctor on a weekly basis. He administered vitamin and mineral drips in his office to fight off the infections. I wasn't seeing much improvement , but I did regain some of my energy. I prayed for a miracle, and a new place to live. I attended a training for my job and met a woman there who took an interest in my work as a public relations professional. She lived in Manhattan and informed me of a cute studio apartment newly remodeled in her midtown neighborhood. I checked it out and quickly relocated there. It was a great location, only four blocks from Rockefeller Center and walking distance to 42nd Street.

During this time my doctor also diagnosed me with chronic fatigue syndrome. So I added that to my list of healing requests. The natural medicine doctor continued treating me with Vitamin C drips and recommended a high protein diet and the total elimination of foods with white flour and sugar. I never knew if this really helped, but I was beginning to feel a little better.

Soon after getting settled in my new place my condition began to improve, and God healed me completely. Now those of you reading this who live in the Bronx, don't get too worried that I'm pointing out this water issue. Many years later I had a similar experience in a rural community just outside of Albany!

9

Defunct Well in the Suburbs

B ecause I was now living in a third world country for several months a year, when I was in the US, I would travel and speak in various places. One summer some friends in the Albany area graciously invited me to live with them and get a little rest for a couple of months while speaking in the area.

It was a beautiful location and great for walking or jogging, surrounded by mountains and only a few miles outside of Albany. After about three weeks I began to have slight symptoms of back pain in the kidney area but ignored it and kept busy.

Upon returning to my adopted country I realized that the symptoms that began in upstate New York were getting worse day by day. After a few months, I returned to Albany. The first thing my friends informed me about was of the discovery of e- coli in their well water. One of them had become seriously ill from it. I inquired as to how they could substantiate that as a fact. The one who was a nurse informed me that she had taken a sample of their water to a lab for analysis. It was a fact. The water was contaminated with E-coli. This was clearly the reason for my symptoms which began to develop during the summer I spent with them.

I believed if God healed me of e-coli before, he could heal me again. I began to pray earnestly for a touch from God. I had prayer at churches and called upon family and friends to pray for my complete healing. Within a few months I was symptom free. I had a complete physical a few months later and my kidneys were normal.

10

No Panacea in Paradise

I was excited to be flying to Hawaii for a special two month training in preparation for work I would be directing in a third world country. The area of Kona was beautiful, serene and absolutely gorgeous! Our classes and workshops would take up most of our days, but we had some evenings free to sit by the ocean and catch the mist as the waves rolled in. Gazing at the ocean, one couldn't help but to reflect on how awesome God is to create so much beauty for our enjoyment.

After about two weeks, I began to feel sick with pain in my abdomen; this became worse each day. H-Pylori bacteria was rampant in the drinking water there. However, no one seemed to be aware of it, or at least if they knew of it, neglected to inform us newcomers.

The daily schedule was very tight. In the morning I did my fitness routine, ate breakfast, and attended classes; after lunch, I worked in the public relations office, providing pro bono consulting services. There were also evening programs at least two or three times a week.

I thought perhaps my feeling poorly was just adjusting to the heavy daily schedule we kept under high humidity in 110 degree weather which I was unaccustomed to.

Saturdays were mostly my day to rest or go sightseeing, hike and explore the surrounding areas such as national parks, etc. Overall, it was a good experience, but my condition was worsening each day.

Finally, one day, after I had been there for about six weeks I went for a blood test. I didn't really understand the results as they never explained anything; they just gave me a paper with some notes. In the meantime I took the paper with the notes to a local health fair. By now I was also experiencing cramping in my back and legs. I didn't know it, but the bacteria was now in my bloodstream.

At the health fair I visited with a doctor about my symptoms and he quickly informed me of H-pylori bacteria being prominent in the water there.

Doctors informed me that they did not have any treatment for the H-pylori bacteria, and that I had a serious ulcer from it eating away my insides. A natural medicine doctor gave me a supplement to help balance my digestive system and make the environment more conducive to healing.

I had to approach God again for healing from contaminated water in Hawaii. At the time, I had no idea I was becoming sicker by the day from the water. Who would have thought that could happen in a surreal place like Hawaii?

I took only about half of the supplement, without any improvement and went home to my mother's home. Upon arrival I continued to pray for God to completely heal me while I rested at home. Two weeks later I was completely recovered! God had done it again! Don't you rejoice that God never tires of us coming to him with our wish list for healing?

11

INTERVENTION IN POISONING CRISIS

L iving in New York City, one can't be surprised at anything! This next account is unbelievable, but it could have been worse without intervention. I was flying from Los Angeles into Newark airport and taking a bus to Port Authority on 42nd Street in New York City.

On the first leg of the trip I had eaten a meal on the flight. I began to feel a little sick, so during my layover I went into an airport chapel to pray. On the last leg of the flight I felt worse, so upon my arrival at Newark, I quickly found my bus and boarded. Once I arrived at Port Authority I could barely stand up due to the severity of the pain! I informed the bus driver of my condition and he called ahead and alerted a Port Authority officer to assist me.

Upon arrival at Port Authority I was met by two kind officers who waited for all the passengers to exit before assisting me off. I informed them that although I felt like I was going to pass out, I didn't need an ambulance. They asked me where I lived and decided that since my apartment was close to a nearby hospital they would just take me. I agreed that would be best. They dropped me off at the hospital.

I approached the desk and explained that I possibly had food poisoning. The lady took my information and told me to have a seat and wait; someone would be with me shortly. There weren't any other patients around, probably due to the lateness of the hour, as it was nearly midnight. I did as I was told and soon a heavy set man barged into the room. He suddenly snatched the folding chair out from under me and muttered something about people not being allowed to sit.

I fell, hitting the floor and landing on my lower back. I was in so much pain I couldn't get up off of the floor. As I looked up he was exiting through another door across the room. The woman at the desk didn't want to be involved, probably afraid of the man. I realized I was lying under a coin-operated pay telephone, as during that time most public places had payphones. I reached up and dialed 911. When they answered I informed them of what had just taken place, and the dispatcher sent a couple of policemen. They searched for the man who had assaulted me but could not locate him.

They went and found a doctor who brought a gurney to put me on and an orderly wheeled me into a hallway. The doctor said they would order X-rays, explaining that I could have a fracture due to what just happened in their hospital. I laid on the gurney for another two hours without being examined by anyone. At that hour of the night in an empty hallway I was beginning to be concerned about security.

I spent the night on the gurney, and no one bothered to check on me to even see if I needed anything. Early the next morning as soon as the office staff came in I inquired about the phone extension for the hospital chaplain. I was able to reach him and explained all that had transpired. He was very concerned and came to my aid immediately.

Soon after an X-ray technician took an X-ray of my back. I wasn't informed of the results. The chaplain was very apologetic although he had not caused the events. He suggested that I contact my city councilman or councilwoman and relate the events to them.

The chaplain advised me to leave the hospital and go home. It was obviously unsafe for me to remain there in the hallway on the gurney since my attacker had not been found yet. The chaplain offered to drive me home, and I accepted. I was weak and my legs wobbly but at least the pain from the food poisoning was subsiding. I managed to walk up the one flight of stairs to my apartment. Once in the flat I dropped onto my bed and began to pray for God to heal my body. I laid there for a couple of days and felt the hand of God touching my body. The symptoms of food poisoning went away until there wasn't any pain, and my back began to align properly until that pain also subsided.

I eventually called one of the city council members. She apologized and immediately took action; I never did receive a bill from the hospital for that night.

12

CHILDLIKE FAITH

L iving in a small close knit community in the Midwest, people become really close friends. Our family had become good friends with a new family who had recently taken over a local business. They had a daughter, Alexis, the same age as my five-year-old daughter Dee.

For most of her adult life, my mother was active planning Christmas programs. As a grandma, she hadn't slowed down, especially around Christmas time. Sometimes I traveled to other places to speak. During one such trip in December, my mother was very busy with the rehearsals for the Christmas program. Upon my return, she and Dee excitedly informed me of the progress of the rehearsals. My mother did, however, mention one thing that was sobering.

She said, "Alexis's mother came carrying her because she couldn't walk."

I thought that was really odd. My mother informed me that it was a mystery as to the reason for the child's inability to walk.

I recalled that the previous Sunday when I picked Alexis up for church, she dragged her feet as she walked. I walked slowly, but she walked even more slowly. I had gently encouraged her to hurry. Of course, I thought it was just child's play. Alexis was a very good child, so I knew she wasn't being rebellious. I assumed she was just playing around a little.

Alexis's parents took her to the city and had her examined by doctors at the Children's Hospital in Denver. They were there for a few days. Upon their return they gave us the negative report from the doctors. It was very bad news. Alexis had been diagnosed with Guillain Barre Syndrome. The prognosis was uncertain.

Her father said, "We will have to wait and see how it progresses. We did learn that there is an injection that might work, but it costs thousands of dollars for one treatment!"

His new business wasn't doing well enough for him to be able to afford a trial like this.

Sometime there are community fundraisers for people with health issues. Since this family was new, that most likely wouldn't happen. A couple of weeks passed, and there was no sign of improvement. At church, Dee requested prayer for her little friend to be healed. She wanted her to get well soon because she missed playing with her. Usually the girls played together once or twice a week.

The church prayed for Alexis, and the following week Dee insisted on going to see her friend. I agreed to take her for a visit. Upon arrival, Dee's mom met us at the door and informed us that Dee was in the kitchen playing with her little two-year-old sister. She had to play on top of the dining room table to keep her little sister from grabbing her toys and tossing them around the room; when that happened, Alexis couldn't run to retrieve them.

Dee ran over to her, and they were so happy to see each other! It was a little uncomfortable for Dee to play with Alexis sitting up on top of the table, but they tried to do the best that they could under the circumstances. Finally, Alexis decided she wanted to get down and play with Dee on the floor. So she called for her mom who carefully placed Alexis on the floor. That was more like previous playdates. They played for a while, and Dee would fetch what little sister threw. That soon grew old.

Dee finally said, " Alexis, we prayed for you in church so you can walk! Go and get that . . ."

Alexis just stood up and went for it. I looked in the direction her mom was looking. Her mom gasped. "WOW! Alexis you are walking!" She turned to me and said, "She has not walked in three weeks!"

We thanked God that day for the Christmas miracle
that Jesus had given to us.

13

GOLDEN GLORY

My daughter and I decided to take a vacation before school began. We had never been to an old fashioned camp meeting together. So, I thought it would be nice to attend the Ward/Heflin Calvary Camp in Virginia. I had traveled to Israel a few years earlier and stayed at the home of the late Ruth Ward Heflin. Now Ruth had returned home to Virginia and was involved in the summer camp meetings.

I had heard of how God was greatly using special speakers like David Herzog, Mahesh Chavda, Jill Austin, Renny McClean, and others. God was doing something special at the camp this summer. There had been talk of the glory of God covering the camp like a cloud!

I thought it would be a good experience for both of us. So I booked the flight and made all the arrangements to attend a week of the camp meeting.

We arrived and began attending the services. The next day we met some of the people who worked at the camp. They told us stories of people having their dental needs met and even of gold fillings showing up in their mouths. One of the women informed me that she was a volunteer at the camp and needed to have a couple of teeth filled. She explained that she lived by faith and couldn't really afford to have the work done by a dentist. She added, "I sure hope tonight is my night to receive the gold fillings!"

How amazing, I thought as I looked at her. I said, "I hope you receive the answer to your prayer."

Later, in the service that evening, I saw the woman I had visited with earlier laughing and rejoicing and running to the front of the sanctuary. I asked her what happened. She opened her mouth and pointed out to me several gold fillings! I returned to my seat next to an elderly woman around eighty-years-old. She, too, was rejoicing and had a mirror looking inside of her mouth. She had said earlier in the day that she had an entire mouth full of rotten teeth! Now she opened her mouth to show me her teeth were all filled with bright yellow gold fillings.

Near the end of the week we rode into town with one of the camp staff who desired to treat us to ice cream and take a ride off the campground. As we talked, I mentioned that I didn't really understand some things about the camp.

He answered all of my questions and then said, "By the way you have gold streaks on your teeth!" He added, "Sometimes the gold fillings begin that way, with tiny streaks that grow larger overtime."

I thought he was just joking, but when I returned to our room, I looked in a mirror. Sure enough, there were gold streaks on my wisdom teeth and a few molars. I laughed and I cried. What had I done to deserve this gold!

My new friend informed me it was God's way of sending a little bit of heaven to earth. You know the streets are gold in heaven. I felt really special!

Now, fast-forward twenty years. I am now living by faith in a third world country and visiting friends in the USA. I have just been to the dentist and had my teeth cleaned and was preparing to return to my adopted country in a few weeks. The dentist had just informed me that a tooth in which I was experiencing some pain had an old filling that was worn down and needed to be replaced. It was one of the molars that had previously been covered with platinum gold at the camp.

Recently I had been reading Ruth Heflin's books on the glory and thought, "Wouldn't it be amazing if I received a restoration of that gold filling while reading the book *Golden Glory*.

I asked the Lord while reading "*Golden Glory*" if he wanted to give me gold in my mouth again. I forgot all about it as I had many things to do to prepare for my trip. It didn't look like I would have time to have the filling restored. When I arrived in my adopted country a few weeks later, I decided to have a chipped tooth repaired as it was right in the front. I had made an appointment prior to my arrival. I went to the dentist office the day after I arrived. Dental fees in these countries are a lot less expensive than in the USA, and many of the dentists in other countries were trained in America.

The dentist repaired the chipped tooth and then I asked her to check the tooth needing a refilling. I also gave her the X-rays and notes from the previous dentist in the USA. She appeared confused and said, "You aren't having any pain in that tooth are you?" She added, "That tooth is fine, and it doesn't look like an old filling."

At that moment I realized that I hadn't had any pain in that tooth for some time! I also remembered asking the lord to refill it with gold. I looked in my purse for a magnifying mirror and looked into my mouth; sure enough, it was filled with platinum gold!

Why would God do something unusual like filling teeth with gold? One can only guess. I believe it is simply one of the signs of his great LOVE for us!

14

THE GREAT PHYSICIAN SPECIALIZES

I call Jesus the Great Physician as there is not a case that he can't heal or is unwilling to heal. He is so grieved over people who have suffered a long time, doing everything their doctors have instructed them to do and yet they suffer even more each day.

Doctors are human, too, and most of them try very hard to see their patients recover.

Sometimes patients put all their faith in general practitioners and specialists, without seeing any progress. When they realize that they may not have long to live, they are reaching out for prayer as a last resort. Sometimes they are miraculously healed on their deathbeds. Other times, I believe Jesus can't stand to see them suffer any more on this earth so he just calls them to their heavenly home! There they receive a new body which is much better than healing the earthly body.

In these next three female cases, each person made a decision as to who to trust with their lives. The outcomes were the same, but all of them learned lessons through their ordeals, mostly to trust God!

God did not orchestrate their dire situations to teach them a lesson as God is good. Only Satan makes people ill, not God. Nevertheless God can take what the devil means for bad and turn it for good for people, in spite of themselves. The first case is about my own answer to prayer.

I had been having slight pain in one of my breasts from a lump and decided to get it checked out. I was examined by a doctor and informed that it was possibly breast cancer. A needle biopsy was taken, and the results were inconclusive. I was advised to treat it as if it was a malignancy. I was informed that I should make an appointment at a women's clinic as soon as possible. The doctor was not required to document this as I was examined at a health fair, and I didn't have health insurance at the time. She and her assistants advised taking out a good health insurance policy right away before I went to the women's clinic as it may be a long road ahead.

I prayed about the course of action I should take. Human reasoning was fighting faith. Should I assume, as they were assuming, that the lump was indeed malignant? Or should I assume it wasn't? I read healing Scriptures and prayed about it daily. I didn't look into health insurance but decided to make an appointment at the women's clinic first for a routine physical as that wasn't very expensive.

I called the clinic and explained my situation and asked for an appointment. There were some problems scheduling me, and they asked me to call back in a few days. I waited a week and called back but still no firm date was set because the appointment date they gave me coincided with another appointment I already had. So I called back and cancelled and tried to set up a new date. The new date ended up being over a month later!

In the meantime, I researched breast disease and how it begins and the optional cures. One day while watching television I came across a Benny Hinn program. He was talking about going to Canada to conduct a healing crusade there. *How nice, that was at least a four hour international flight for me. The trip would be too expensive for me to budget for.*

I waited for him to announce his upcoming USA schedule, but he never did. It seemed the only crusade scheduled was the one in Canada.

At that moment, God spoke to me and said, "You are going to that crusade in Canada!"

A couple of hours later, Peggy, a friend from Canada, called me.

She said, "I have something to tell you, but first you must agree to say yes to the proposal I have for you!"

I reluctantly said, "Okay, yes. But how can I agree to something when I don't know what I'm agreeing to?"

But I knew God was up to something! She said, "When I was in church this morning the Lord spoke to me and told me to buy you a plane ticket to come here to Toronto. Benny Hinn is coming here, and you are to be in that meeting! I already bought your ticket just this afternoon."

I almost fell off the sofa. I told her what the Lord had just told me that afternoon. So I was off to Canada in a few weeks.

Upon arrival we went straight to the Benny Hinn meeting and found good seats where we could see and hear everything easily. As soon as Hinn stood up, one of the first things he said was, "There are many people here tonight who have a problem in their breast, and God wants to heal you tonight! Run to the front and as you are coming, God will touch you."

I informed Peggy of my situation, and she encouraged me to go to the front. I did and afterwards Hinn's people took us to a room where we met with the crusade doctors who asked us questions and wrote down all of our information. They promised to follow up with us. They said sometimes symptoms left immediately and other times it took awhile but not to be discouraged, just keep believing!

After we left the meeting and went to my friend's house, I kept feeling the lump and noticed it was still the same size. Peggy said I was showing a lack of faith when I kept checking it.

She said, "Just forget about it and stop feeling and checking it. God will do it as he has healed you already. When you are not thinking about it, one day it will disappear."

I took her advice and decided to enjoy my stay in Toronto that week. It is a city that I love to visit because it's so clean and beautiful.

True to their word, the Benny Hinn people had called me immediately following the crusade to encourage me to keep on believing God for my healing. They prayed for me over the phone for the healing to be completed. They were nice compassionate people, really showing the love of God.

In the meantime, I had researched breast health and diet. I changed my diet as well to eat less fat and more fruits and vegetables and fewer carbs. I also added maitake and reishi mushrooms with a combination of natural herbs that improve breast health. I believe we should do what we need to do to maintain healthy bodies, and God will do the rest.

I don't know when it happened, but one day after I returned home, the lump disappeared.

15

SURGERY CANCELLED
FOR CHOIR DIRECTOR

While living in New York City I spent weekends involved in activities assisting others. Most Saturdays were spent volunteering at a youth juvenile detention facility, mentoring teenage girls. Sundays were spent at an inner city church doing whatever needed to be done to assist the pastor and ministry. One of the activities that I loved to do was pray for the sick.

One particular Sunday I was asked to pray for the choir director, Christy, a lovely lady who really had a deep relationship with Jesus. She was always pleasant and her face just kind of glowed. She informed me that she had recently been diagnosed with breast cancer and was to have surgery that coming week. I asked her if she believed God wanted to heal her as Jesus had paid the price with his blood The Bible says that by his stripes (wounds from beatings) we're healed. She said, "Yes, I do believe that he wants to heal me."

I asked her if she was willing to request that the tests be repeated before allowing any surgery. She said, "Yes, I' m willing to do that."

I prayed for her and felt the presence of God come upon us as we prayed. It was an overshadowing of his love accompanied by his power. She also felt it and said that she believed she was healed.

The next week at church her cousin rushed up to me and said, "Thank you for praying for Christy. She went in for the surgery and requested the tests to be retaken and after she was retested, all the tests came back negative. They couldn't find any trace of the lumps or cancer!

We all rejoiced and thanked Jesus for what he had done in her life.

16

DRIED UP AT THE ROOTS

I was back in the Midwest and visiting one of my cousins who was very close to my mother. Actually my mother and Lily were like sisters. They talked on the phone almost daily and visited almost weekly. They were always there for each other, ever since they married and began their families.

My mother had informed me that Lily had a medical issue and wanted me to go to her house and pray with her. Her adult children desired for her to go down south and undergo surgery, but she was hesitant to do so. However, her diagnosis was not good. Neither was the prognosis, so her children were anxious and wanted to eradicate the problem as quickly as possible.

I went to visit Lily and pray for her. There were many people coming and going with a lot of interruptions so it was awhile before I could really sit down and pray. Finally I began to pray for her, not really understanding the situation. When we were interrupted again, I stopped praying and waited as I wanted to pray for her before she went to the hospital.

Lily explained to me that she had been diagnosed with endometrial cancer and would most likely have to undergo a hysterectomy. She planned to go to a hospital close to her adult children and get a second opinion. I ask her if she believed Jesus could heal her and was willing to heal her and she said yes. I told her I would continue to pray for her but asked her to please forgo surgery until she had re-confirmed the diagnosis. She was a rather large woman and doctors had hesitated in the past to do any type of surgery on her because her heart was a little weak.

I prayed for Lily, "Dear Lord, please dry this cancer up at the root. In Jesus name! Amen."

I had just finished praying when another person came in to visit her, so I left her home. A short time later, I discovered her daughter had come and taken her out of state. I hoped she remembered my advice as I didn't have another chance to visit with her again after the prayer.

A couple of weeks later my mother called me and informed me that Lily had called her. Lily was doing well, considering all she had been through. She had not required the doctors to redo the exam, but they simply reviewed the previous tests done in her home state and decided to operate and remove the cancer by a hysterectomy. Lily said that when she was in recovery the surgeons told her, "When we opened you up, that cancer had dried up at the roots! We didn't really need to do a hysterectomy!"

When visiting with my mother, Lily said, "I should have insisted they redo all the tests, especially the ultra sound."

Lily was recovering nicely, and doctors had advised her to receive treatment for an underactive thyroid as well, as it was causing her to be overweight.

17

TUMORS SHRINK AND CALCIFY

I was excited to be starting a brand new job in economic development on the county level in a Midwestern community known to be progressive. I had been doing this work for a few years and knew the drawbacks of trying to develop in an area where the people were not ready for change. My previous employer didn't provide health insurance, so I was ripe for a medical checkup. The new position required me to wait at least three months before the health insurance would be effective. It wasn't a problem as I was in perfect health and had no symptoms of being otherwise.

Most days I worked from 8 am to 5 pm as I wanted to make a difference in this community and provide more jobs by recruiting new businesses. With early morning meetings and evening meetings at least once or twice a week, plus travel, I could feel my body begin to run down. I decided to have a check- up scheduled as soon as my insurance kicked in. I had also noticed a lump in my abdomen, accompanied by slight pain.

Finally the appointment day came, and I went to see Dr. Lundquist. She was very efficient, warm, friendly, and compassionate. She was one of the best doctors I have ever had. She examined me thoroughly. She called in another doctor to also examine my abdomen, and he concurred with her that yes, there was definitely a foreign mass of some kind, a lump in my abdomen. She ordered an ultra sound of my pelvic area.

I made a follow up appointment, and when I returned for the test results the doctor informed me that my body was very healthy, and that lump was a benign fibroid tumor. She said most people just wanted them taken out, and she recommended that I do likewise as this one was the size of an orange. She also informed me that the hospital she was affiliated with didn't do these types of surgeries at this time and suggested I travel to a larger city hospital such as a University Medical Center. She also thought it could possibly be two fibroids—perhaps one laying on top of the other that couldn't be seen clearly.

I researched fibroid tumors and discovered there were several options, One of the options, uterine embolization, was not all that invasive. At least there would be no cutting, sutures, or stitches. In this embolization method, a cauterization specialist (surgeon) simply went up inside of a main artery and cut off the blood supply to the tumor. It seemed simple enough, and one only had to spend one night in the hospital for observation. There were also the options of laser surgery and the standard hysterectomy.

I really didn't have complete peace about any of the options, but chose what I thought was the least risky. I met with the surgeon, and she answered all of my questions and agreed to meet all of my requests during the procedure. The night before the procedure I had quite a bit of anxiety. I called a couple of friends and they prayed with me. They both advised that I undergo the procedure since I had excellent medical insurance. One also said that I should ask the Lord to cancel it or create a situation where I couldn't have the procedure. They all prayed that God would perform a miracle and heal me by dissolving the tumor. We prayed for God's will to be done the next day at the hospital.

I arrived at the hospital early in the morning and filled out the paperwork, signed all of the releases and was prepped for the procedure, which was to begin around 12 noon. I was informed the surgeon would be coming in late, around 1:30 p.m., as she had several emergencies that morning. She arrived closer to 2 p.m. and checked everything to be sure I was prepped properly. Suddenly, before she could begin, her beeper went off and she was called out. She had another patient that was bleeding out and near death, so she immediately left to attend to that patient.

She returned around 3:30 p.m., and just as she was sitting down to begin my procedure, she was called out for another emergency and quickly left. Another specialist offered to do the procedure, but I declined, stating that my surgeon and I had agreed upon specific measures to be followed during the procedure that would protect my organs from receiving unnecessary continuous radiation, during the surgeon's breaks.

Now it was almost 6 p.m., and my surgeon entered the room looking exhausted. She asked me if I wanted to go for the procedure now or return the next day. I could tell she didn't really want to go forward with the procedure this late in the day, and she looked like she was totally drained from her hectic day. She informed me that she had been going non-stop since 6 a.m. that morning. So I opted for the next day.

She said, "It makes no sense to spend an extra night in the hospital since we have done nothing for you today. It's best for you to go home and return in the morning." I totally agreed.

As I was getting dressed in my street clothes, a little voice spoke to me. "Now I am giving you the opportunity to forgo this procedure and just allow me to heal you."

I know the voice of God. Early the next morning, I called the surgeon's office and cancelled the procedure, apologizing profusely to her assistant.

The assistant informed me that this is not a procedure to have performed hastily and said there was no need for an apology.

She went on to say, "A day or two after discharge from the hospital following this procedure, some women visited the ER due to extreme pain they were experiencing." She added, "Most of them had been forced to undergo an emergency hysterectomy due to inflammation and infection!"

I conducted additional research and discovered that most women having success with the embolization procedure had very tiny fibroids, and others had a combination of embolization and laser surgery within an hour of the procedure to prevent infection. I had suggested the laser immediately following my procedure, but my surgeon wouldn't consider it. I continued to research and prayed often about my condition, searching for a solution.

I found a fibroid support group online that a friend recommended. I learned about two additional treatments. I decided to try the option that several in the fibroid support group had experienced success with and the one that offered the least risk. It was a natural medicine that could be taken in a liquid form, and it actually reduced the size of many women's fibroids. The downside of having the fibroid was that it caused heavy menstrual cycles. This liquid would also help to regulate that issue by shrinking the tumor.

After about a year, it was time for me to travel overseas to do some humanitarian work for women and girls in a third world country. I decided that since the fibroid tumors were under control I would take the trip. At least I wasn't experiencing any heavy bleeding. All was going really well until about seven months into the project when I began to suffer with heavy bleeding. I wondered if I could remain there much longer.

I ordered the liquid that had helped before. I would begin taking it again. In the meantime, while waiting a week for it to arrive, I wondered if I had anything on hand that I could take that would stop the bleeding immediately. I had a cabinet full of natural medicine, herbs, and vitamins. The chasteberry just seemed to stand out, so I read about it and began to take it three times a day. To my surprise, the first day I took it, the heavy bleeding stopped. By the time the other liquid arrived, I had everything under control again.

I continued to do research about eventually having the fibroids removed. I worked with a surgeon in Atlanta, Georgia, who had developed a special two-part procedure to minimize the risk of complications of fibroid removal. He and I worked out a financial arrangement, and after six months I was to see him and undergo his procedure.

By the time I returned to the US about six months later, the fibroids had shrunk down to the size of golf balls. I had three ultrasounds which showed that they were shrinking more and more. In the meantime, I met healing evangelist Randy Clark who prayed for me. He encouraged me to keep believing God as he had witnessed another woman receive complete healing of the same condition. God totally healed me. Doctors were surprised and said that they had never seen anything like this happen with fibroids. They asked me what procedures and treatments I had taken. I informed them I didn't have any procedures, and they were amazed.

Doctors looked at the ultra sound results and said, "You will never need to have any treatments or surgery for fibroids ever!"

18

NEW LUNGS FOR A PRODIGAL

I had just returned from an overseas trip and I was attempting to clean up my house and yard. My cousin Mike, who lived a few blocks away, stopped by and offered to help me clean up the yard and do some repairs as he usually did upon my return home. Today, he seemed preoccupied and in deep thought.

A couple of days later Mike came over, mowed grass, trimmed a couple of trees, helped stack dead tree limbs, and basically cleaned up and carried them to the landfill. Again, he appeared to be troubled. I didn't want to pry but wondered what was worrying him. I asked about his family, and he informed me they were well.

Mike notified me that he wasn't going to be able to help much the next week as he was taking a trip to the city for a few days. Most people in this community usually travel to the city for medical issues as rural medicine is not really a priority for doctors these days. I asked him if anything was wrong, and he said, "No, just going to the city."

About a week later Mike returned and stated that he would like to visit with me about a medical report.

I said, "Sure, that would be fine. Just come by anytime."

He usually walks two or three miles a day, always on the same route, taking him on the road in front of my house, so it would be easy for him to drop in anytime. I knew what time he usually finished his walk and passed my house on his way home, so I kept looking for him. I looked at my watch and realized it had been over an hour since he would have taken his usual walk past my house. I knew that most days, after his walk, he had a specific time to deliver "Meals on Wheels" to elderly shut-ins in the community.

I was planning to drive to the city early the next day in the morning so I wouldn't hit rush hour. The next day I didn't see any sign of Mike taking his usual walk past my house. I needed to be on the highway within an hour. I wondered if Mike had already left to do his volunteer work. Since he didn't stop in, I decided I would just leave and be on my way. But no, that little voice of God within me was saying that I really needed to see Mike today.

I thought I'd stop at his house on the way out. I had about fifteen minutes to chat with him, so I went to his house. He was preparing to leave, so I stopped him at the door and asked him if I could pray for him for whatever the issue was that he was facing. He still didn't reveal the nature of the health issue.

He said, "I don't feel I am worthy of you praying for me. I haven't lived my life in the best way. Maybe God wants to punish me."

I said, "God still loves you and wants the best for you." He's not going to strike you with something to punish you for your mistakes. He wants me to pray for you."

Since we didn't have much time, I put my hand on his shoulder and began to pray. Then God told me to begin praying for his lungs. I sensed that God really wanted to touch him and prayed for his lungs specifically. We both had to leave, so I quickly said goodbye and left him standing in the doorway.

A week later I called him to see how he was doing. He informed me that he had been diagnosed with lung cancer several weeks before and the prognosis wasn't good. He had visited with doctors, and now he was scheduled to see a cancer specialist the next day. I informed him that I was sure God had healed him and that he was not to take any negative talk from the doctors to heart. That would allow fear to come into his soul. I explained that we didn't want fear and unbelief to enter his heart. He agreed to follow my advice.

He had the tests retaken, most likely the third time for some. These tests were primarily to determine the best treatment for his case. He had been given options that weren't very acceptable such as cutting out a good percentage of his lung and living on oxygen the rest of his life. There were other formidable choices equally as devastating.

Two weeks later all the test results were sent to him and the paperwork showed negative for lung cancer. He was given a prescription for antibiotics. He said he had been taking them and coughing up lots of junk from his lungs. I advised him to continue taking the antibiotics since his lungs seemed to be clearing itself of the cancer. He took the full course, returned to the doctor a couple of weeks later, and was pronounced cured.

It has been a couple of years now and Mike is still cancer free. Sometime later he told me that when I prayed for him he felt heat come over his body in the lung area. God heals, and he doesn't just choose to heal the people who lived right or deserve healing. God heals those whom he loves, regardless of whether they have made mistakes in their lives. He desires to display his love to everyone.

19

AN ANGEL DEMONSTRATES
THE CURE

I awoke at 1:30 a.m. I had a badly sprained ankle, and it was swollen so much that I couldn't bend it. I went to bed that night moaning and groaning in pain as it throbbed. I had tried everything to get the swelling to go down, i.e. heat packs and ice packs, but nothing seemed to be working.

When I woke up at 1:30 a.m., I was still half asleep and trying to go back to sleep. But I couldn't because the pain had increased. I suddenly remembered my dream of an angel holding a slice of cut garlic to my ankle.

What was that all about? I wondered.

I thought maybe it was a message from God, answering my desperate prayers.

I hobbled to the kitchen as I always kept garlic on hand. I cut up several thin slices and taped them over the most swollen areas of my ankle. Then I wrapped the ace bandage around it, went back to bed, and finally fell asleep.

When I woke up six hours later, I realized I was pain free! I quickly removed the ace bandage, and to my amazement, the swelling had disappeared. I could actually rotate my ankle. God had indeed healed me with instructions from his angel.

20

THE FAITH OF TEENS

I had been working on one of my writing projects and doing fundraising for my nonprofit organization.

On this particular day I was very focused on my writing and deep in thought for several hours. What I didn't realize was that I had been sitting on my foot without moving for a long period of time. I jumped up without even thinking and fell flat on my face. My foot was totally asleep! As I stood up, my foot rolled to the side causing me to fall. Because I couldn't feel my foot, I didn't have any balance.

I suspected that my foot may have fractured due to the quick movement and pressure upon it. I went to see a doctor after a couple of days as we were to leave in a week to take my mother for an extended visit with my brother. I was also scheduled to travel overseas within two or three weeks.

My doctor referred me to a foot specialist, stating, "I'm pretty sure your foot is broken. I'd rather have the foot specialist take the X-rays, so she can determine the extent of your injuries."

I quickly made an appointment with the podiatrist office. The podiatrists examined my foot and took several X-rays. Both ladies were very proficient in their field. They recommended I wear a foot brace for more stability and strength. They said my foot was not fractured but seriously sprained. The ligaments on the side of the foot were also injured.

One of the doctors said, "I don't think you will be traveling anywhere soon!" She added, "This type of injury can take up to six weeks to heal."

Two weeks later, it was time for us to travel to Kansas City. My mother and I flew there. My brother met us at the airport. Previously, my family had visited the International House of Prayer and enjoyed our time there. I decided to attend a service while visiting my daughter who was enrolled in classes there.

That particular night during the worship time, students were praying for people all over the building. A couple of teenage girls saw my brace and asked about my injury. They requested permission to pray for my foot, and I quickly agreed. I explained to them that I planned to be traveling in a week. They believed that God would heal my foot in time for me to travel and to travel without the brace.

"WOW!" I said. "That sounds great!"

They prayed for my foot and asked me to wiggle my toes to see if I still had any pain. I still had some pain, especially when I moved my foot. They continued to pray and finally said they felt that it was healed.

The next morning, I removed the brace and got out of bed. As I put my foot down on the floor I realized my foot was healed; there wasn't any pain.

I praised God for the healing. In about a week I was ready to take my international flight, and I didn't need the brace. I never put it back on after that day. My trip was without incident, and my foot didn't even fatigue or feel sore upon my arrival. God does a complete job when he heals!

OUR THIRD WORLD COUNTRY HEALINGS

My daughter and I are people of adventure and like to experience new things. While living in a third world country high up in the Himalayan Mountains, we were exposed to many challenges as there wasn't always medical care available immediately when needed. We saw the hand of God work in healing of our bodies several times. I will mention a few of the cases here so you can have some idea of what we were up against. There were other times that if you were in the right place at the right time, you received medical treatment equal to or superior to the care we received in the USA.

21

MALARIA IN THE MOUNTAINS AND VALLEYS

The region where we lived in Asia was known for malaria; some areas were worse than others. Certain times of the year, especially in spring and summer, there were heavy monsoon rains that increased the mosquito population and transmitted malaria into the area. A time came when I needed to travel to one of the high-risk malaria areas of the plains. I forgot that this area was a high-risk malaria area at the time, as I was traveling in the spring. I was planning to fly there early in the morning and return in the evening. Well, the trip didn't go as planned, and I ended up being in the area several days, near a swamp full of mosquitoes.

By the end of the day I had a number of mosquito bites, but I didn't think much of it until night time when my host gave me a mosquito net to cover the bed. The little critters still managed to get inside the net and bite me unmercifully. By morning I was covered head to toe with bites. I was also running a fever and beginning to feel a little ill. My host recommended an ointment, but all the stores in the area were sold out.

After a few days I finally was able to acquire the ointment my host had recommended. By the time I returned home, four days had passed. I was getting really sick and had used up all the ointment. I was miserable. Then I realized since my fever was getting higher daily that I had most likely contracted malaria from all those mosquito bites.

Several years earlier, I had taken chloroquinine with me on a couple of trips to Asia for prevention of malaria. Now I didn't have any of those pills with me. This was also my first time traveling to one of the high risk malaria areas. I began to pray for healing. Within a week my body miraculously recovered. All my symptoms disappeared as quickly as they had come.

22

ACID IN THE EYES?

My daughter, Dee, and I had been aiding a couple of children's homes financially, and as a student, she was helping the children learn English. One day we were invited to meet the group at a place that was new to us. Most houses are two-story and sometimes people just drop things or pour liquids from the second floor onto people walking on the sidewalk below. One has to be keenly aware of his surroundings. As we entered the courtyard, something unseen blew into my eyes. It felt like a liquid. I tried to wipe my eyes with my sleeves, hoping it would just go away, but it didn't.

We went inside, and my daughter interacted with the children. I knew that I couldn't wash my eyes out with any water there as it contained very high levels of bacteria. Some foreigners have had serious incurable infections just from shaving with the tap water. I ended up sitting in a dark room while the others played games and had a great time. The pain increased in my eyes by the hour.

We finally left and returned to our flat. I washed my eyes out with a saline solution I had in my first aid kit. That seemed to help a little, but the burning persisted. By now my vison was getting blurry. The next morning my eyes were even more blurry. I continued to pray for an answer to my problem.

I called a friend and asked if she had heard of anything like what I was experiencing. She stated that it could most likely be acid and recommended that I go to a famous eye hospital in the area which I had never heard of.

I made an appointment and went early the next morning. By morning the pain had decreased substantially and the blurred vision was also less noticeable. My vision was becoming clearer. By the time I arrived and was seen by a doctor, it was two hours later, and after undergoing a series of tests and exams, I was prescribed eye drops for dry eyes. I thank God for restoring my eyes. Unfortunately, in certain areas of Southeast Asia, there are quite a number of random acid attacks upon women.

23

FACIAL DEFORMITY HEALED

I n three days I was scheduled to speak at a gathering. I looked in the mirror at my swollen blistered face and wondered if I should cancel. The thought occurred to me that it would be too late for them to acquire another person to fill in my time. Then I thought about Jesus's face with the blood running down it from the crown of thorns. How dare I be ashamed of my face!

I decided to go through with the engagement. I tried many types of medications, but nothing was working. It appeared as a rash and shingles on my face. The affected side of my face even drooped a little. I continued to pray for a solution and kept trying various essential oils and creams. I finally decided to just let it be and continue praying about it.

The morning of the meeting I covered my face with two bandages as I didn't want to frighten the people by my appearance I ended up falling down a flight of stairs on my way out the door. Well, I thought, could it really get any worse? Now I'm limping in pain as well as sporting a bandaged face.

When I entered, everyone close to the door asked, "What happened to your face?"

I said, "It's nothing to worry about."

They just stared at me with frightened looks on their faces. In third world countries, every physical ailment is something to worry about as people die quickly from unknown afflictions. At the end of the day, a friend suggested I go to a hospital and try a locally manufactured medication.

 It just so happened that the next day, when I went to a hospital, a dermatologist was actually that very day, having traveled six hours. He usually did this trip every week or two. He stated my problem looked like one only found in this region and could only be treated by the local medicine. He gave me the locally manufactured cream to use for a week. In a few days my face was healed. It was a miracle I didn't have any scars remaining from the infection.

24

SOUR GRAPES

In certain parts of Asia people have always warned, "Beware of the grapes! Do not eat the grapes!"

In the fall, street vendors seem to be everywhere with their carts piled high with lovely large dark purple grapes. They were priced unreasonably low, also, and this bunch looked so inviting! After passing up the grapes for several years I decided I would eat them just this one time.

I took them to the place I was staying and rinsed them in iodine-treated water. I was staying in a guest house, preparing for a meeting that would take place in that city after three days. They did not disappoint as they were fat, juicy, and sweet.

The next morning I was in trouble from eating the grapes; I was bleeding as I urinated and my bladder was inflamed! I immediately went to the hospital and after a two hour wait, was seen by a woman doctor.

In Asia, we carry our own medical records with us whenever we enter a clinic or hospital. The doctor reviewed the ultrasound of my old films showing little dots like peas where fibroid tumors had shrunken years before. She inquired about the small dots.

"What did you do about the fibroids? Did you have surgery?"

I said, "No, I took a few drops of a natural medicine and prayed a lot and was healed."

She said, "That's a miracle!"

I had an ultra sound that she ordered and stayed at the hospital all day waiting for the results. Finally around 6 p.m., I was informed that the doctor had the diagnosis. She said it might be a slight kidney and bladder infection. In preparing for the ultrasound, I prayed that any inflammation would clear out when I drank the two liters of water required for the ultra sound. God did just that, and at the end of the day, no inflammation was seen on any of the tests. Two days later I attended my meetings, and all went well. The symptoms never returned.

25

THE TRIP FROM HELL

I had made this trip to Asia many times but felt a little uneasy as tensions were increasing between one particular Asian country and the USA. I had changed my ticket to change planes in Hong Kong instead of the mainland. This was one of those rare times I was traveling without comfortable shoes. I had just left a conference and hadn't brought comfortable shoes. It was to only be an hour layover.

Unfortunately, my flight was delayed and arrived 30 minutes late at the transfer point. My assigned seat had been given to another passenger. It was a nightmare trying to rebook a ticket out of Hong Kong. I was given the run around and asked to relinquish my passport, which I refused to do.

Finally after six hours going from counter to counter and searching for my checked luggage, I was forced to take a flight to another destination and fly from there to my final destination the next day. I had walked all over the airport and my feet were becoming very sore. I obtained a hotel room at the airport and rested for four hours before boarding my flight early the next morning.

For weeks and months after my arrival at my final destination my feet were swollen and painful. I discovered I had acquired planter fasciitis, most likely from the airport fiasco. I tried creams and exercises, but to no avail. It appeared surgery was a likely option, but I wasn't ready to consider that yet.

One day a friend suggested I go to a hospital where she worked and have X-rays taken. I went there but unfortunately the X-ray technician was out due to a holiday. My friend and I prayed for a few patients and by the time we left there my foot pain of over a month was subsiding. During the next few days my pain completely left and I was healed and could walk normally again. I even began walking my usual two or three miles per day.

HEALING SUMMARY

When we talk about biblical healings and the works of Jesus, people want to see a theology. There really isn't a theology on healing for one to study. In a university study done many years ago, and in subsequent studies, it was discovered that patients receiving prayer during their health crisis were healed at a much higher rate than those without prayer.

Let's take a quick overview of the history of divine health. In the Old Testament, the children of Israel wandered in the desert for forty years and they were in good health, not one sick among them. Even Moses did not die of illness in his old age.

Our human reasoning and logic isn't always the best way to good health, but our words release the presence of God into the atmosphere. God spoke and the world was created. We must pray for wisdom as to how we should be speaking, especially when in the middle of a crisis.

Colossians 3:2 says that we are to set our minds on things above, heavenly things, not on earthly things. This is where faith comes into the picture. In the Old Testament, when one touched a leper, he became unclean. In the New Testament, when Jesus touched a leper, the leper was healed. The healing power is in the stripes (wounds) of Jesus.

We must apply the blood of Jesus when we are seeking healing of the body. Having a greater understanding of healing increases one's faith. The Holy Spirit brings the revelation of God's promises and how to apply them to our lives.

Why is the blood that Jesus shed so very important? The blood of an infant comes from the father. Jesus blood was created from Yahweh, the Father in heaven. The Holy Spirit came upon Mary and she conceived. Upon this earth Jesus also lived a sinless life of purity and holiness. His blood wasn't defiled in any way.

The blood of Jesus is THE most powerful element, like an atomic bomb going off in the spiritual realm. I celebrate and give Jesus all the glory for all the healings in my family. These healings were only possible due to the horrendous suffering of Jesus at the hands of the Roman soldiers—thirty-nine stripes, tearing open his back and ripping his flesh, muscles, tendons ,and ligaments, creating deep wounds out of which his pure blood flowed! God's word is like medicine for your body, soul, and spirit.

Some people think that it's the length of the prayers, but that is not the most important. It is where you put your trust that is important. If we fully trust in God, we can give him our spirit, soul, and body. Hebrews 11:6 says that we must walk in faith, as without it we can't please God. Try not to be with people who only speak doomsday to your situation.

God frees our body, soul, and spirit. Faith belongs to the law of life. Faith in Jesus removes the *spirit of fear*, as it is the opposite of fear. Fear causes people to absorb what is around them. If fearful, tell it to GO! It may rear its ugly head again, but keep telling it to go.

Remind yourself of John 20:29. Blessed are those who believe even though they don't see it. Mark 11:23 says that if we have faith we can move mountains. Romans 4:17 tells us how to build up our faith to fully trust God. We call those things that are not as though they are already there.

By HIS stripes you are healed. Do you believe it?

I recommend the following books for you to read:

- *Heavenly Authority* by John Lake
- *The Power of Faith* by Smith Wigglesworth

Apostle Paul says, "The law of the spirit of life in Christ Jesus, hath made me free from the law of sin and death" (Romans 8:2 KJV).

John 6:63 says that Christ's words are "spirit and life," that the Spirit quickens. 1 John 4:4 says that "He who is in you is greater than he who is in the world." You have authority from heaven to tread upon the enemy. Nothing can hurt you, so be bold. "God has not given us a spirit of fear, but of power and of love and of a sound mind" (2 Tim. 1:7 NKJV). Three in one are the Father, Son, and Holy Spirit. Holy Spirit is a spirit of power, love, and a sound mind.

Laugh at the enemy! Sickness has no power over you. You have dominion in Christ (Luke 9:1-6). You have power over the unclean to cast out sickness and disease brought about by evil spirits. The power of God is in your spirit. Believe it and stand on it. Believe you have received the answer to your prayers. People who stand together and trust God are powerful in the Spirit.

"John G. Lake, a leader in the Pentecostal movement that began in the early 20th century, is known as a faith healer [and] missionary . . . His main vision was to train others to walk in the power of God."[2] John Lake prayed over his dead sister. He said, "This thing is of hell, it cannot and it will not be! In the name of Jesus I abolish sickness and death and she shall live!"

She resurrected. It is not the length of the prayers but believing that God will answer. Yet sometimes it takes praying all night to see the answer.[3]

Holy Spirit is our helper and he prays with us as we are united. When John Lake went to Africa, he took communion every day. Germs couldn't live in his body. Genesis 1:6 says God gave man dominion. Take every thought captive and obey Jesus, keeping your mind on God. It is a creative work. Everything God created was good.

Direct the power of God, which is the Holy Spirit, to the body part that needs healing; demand it to function as God created it to function.

We separate ourselves to live pure. If we fall, Jesus has come to restore us. He died to redeem our bodies and soul. James 5:13-15 says if anyone is sick, anoint him with oil and pray. Our confidence comes from knowing Jesus.

Healing evangelist Kathryn Kuhlman didn't claim to have a special gift of healing. She honored the Holy Spirit; God's presence and healing was released in her meetings. Kuhlman didn't have healing lines as people were healed sitting in the audience. She said, "What I have is something any Christian could have if he would pay the price of full surrender and yieldedness. I'm absolutely dependent on the mercy of the Lord."[4]

One important element in praying for the sick is compassion. Jesus showed compassion. The Good Samaritan story is an example (Luke 10:25-37). Widow of Nain's son's resurrection is also an example (Luke 7:11-17).

Sometimes you must fight for the healing. John Lake prayed for sixteen hours for a man to be healed and delivered from morphine. His friend came and joined him in prayer. Finally, the man was healed. It always helps to have a friend pray, too.

Sometimes we're tested. Jesus was tested forty days after he was baptized in the Jordon River. During that time, the enemy tested him. Jesus was a threat to Satan. That is the reason Satan also tests us. We're a threat to him. Jesus returned in the power of the Holy Spirit. So can we, leaning on Jesus and the Holy Spirit. On earth Jesus was the son of man, like us, and he surrendered to the Holy Spirit.

Jesus did miracles at the direction of his father in heaven. He received instructions when he went away to pray. He sent the Holy Spirit for us to do the same works he did and greater. In Acts we see that soon after the Holy Spirit came, Peter and John went to the temple. What happened? The lame man was healed.

We must be dedicated fully to Jesus. Give your body, soul, and spirit—all to Jesus.

Our emotions are a part of our soul. Since feelings and behavior follow our thoughts, we must guard our thoughts diligently. We must be sure we are basing our thoughts, decisions, and feelings on truth found only in Scripture. The Word of God is medicine for our soul, body, and spirit. We need to read it every day.

God will reward us. Jesus had no place to lay his head, and sometimes, we may have needs, too, but we must be strong in the power of the Holy Spirit as Jesus was. How much do we want to see a move of God? Do we really want it? Ask God to give you the gifts of healing and miracles. When you get it, be careful, as people will lift you up and praise you. Always give God **all** the glory.

Many years ago, God used one man to begin a spiritual awakening in the United States. He prayed five hours every day for two and a half years, then he went up to seven hours a day for a year and a half. His name was William J. Seymour. He was a waiter in a hotel and pastored a congregation.

The awakening was called The Azuza Street Revival. Although many unusual healings and miracles took place during this time, Seymour suffered hatred and mistreatment from people who criticized him. He was a very humble man. They were jealous because God was using him mightily. He was a simple man without an education. People actually stole his ministry mailing list from him. God used him in a mighty way.[5]

When Seymour preached in a church of 10,000 people, Lake said Seymour became glorified. Men shook and trembled and cried out to God. Lake did not believe any other man in modern times had such a wonderful deluge of God in his life![6]

You can't depend on man, but Jesus gives you the desires of your heart. Jesus is the miracle worker and healer who makes a way for us. He is the greatest doctor. Remember, if you have accepted Jesus as your Lord and Savior, he lives in you. He loves you and guides you by the Holy Spirit's presence. Most people only live by what they see in the natural.

In the past, maybe you have tried to pray in faith and were disappointed at the outcome. Maybe you believed God, but your situation remained unchanged. So you began to think that your faith didn't produce results, or at least not the result you were hoping for.

Now you are afraid to believe God again, as you experienced suffering, sorrow, and pain. The enemy attacked your mind and emotions. But we must know that God is omniscience and omnipotent. He is all knowing, ultimate wisdom and all powerful.

Divine healing is the seal of God's acknowledgement, the proof to the world that Jesus is the Son of God.[7]

This is where Romans 8:28 comes in as we trust God to fulfill this promise. "All things work together for good for those who are called according to his purpose in Christ Jesus." In this next scenario, I saw a little glimpse of the other side and had to trust God no matter how difficult.

OPEN THE GATES

The memory of that cold winter day will always be in my thoughts.

My brother Nathan was born developmentally disabled from lack of oxygen when a doctor had sent our mother home just before the birth. Knowing it would take nearly an hour to return, he misjudged the situation. Nathan was born in the car on the trip back to the hospital.

Lack of oxygen caused his brain to develop inadequately, and he was born borderline mentally retarded. He also suffered seizures as a result of the traumatic birth. Most people did not understand his disability as it was hidden except in a classroom and in social situations.

Now, as an adult, it appeared that my brother had been the victim of a horrific crime, most likely due to his disability. No one could explain to my family what had happened.

I remained near Nathan's bed in ICU around the clock except for leaving briefly and returning with worship music. Some say comatose patients can hear. Therefore, I spoke to him softly and played the music off and on all day. He moved his lips, trying to respond.

Doctors had given up all hope; however, I believed for a miracle. At 2:30 am, the power and presence of the living God filled the room. I sensed that Nathan was breathing on his own.

At that moment, the respiratory technician entered the room, checked the respirator, and said, "Yes, surprisingly, he is breathing over the respirator now."

Nathan was back, but God did not want him to suffer anymore. Two days later at 4:45 am, as I slept off and on by Nathan's bedside, I awoke and opened my Bible. It fell open to Psalms 89: "I made a covenant with you my chosen one . . . a promise from God."

Nathan was like the biblical David, as he loved to sing and play the guitar. He could easily pick up a tune, as that was one of his gifts from God. In summary, God was saying, "He is mine".

I stood and prayed over him, and suddenly, I had a vision of Nathan near the gates of heaven.

Suddenly, I could hear the heavenly Father's voice commanding, "Open the gates! Open the gates, let him come in. Bring him to me. Welcome home! Come and let me love you, my son. I want to hold you in my arms."

What a grand welcome! My brother was now safe at home resting in the arms of his heavenly Father. The vision ended. The presence of God flooded the room. I was surrounded by angels.

The song, "Where I Belong" came on the radio, sung by Building 429. It speaks of going home to a place where you will be accepted. The blessed assurance is that one day all of God's children are going home where we belong.

The Holy Spirit can show you reality from God's perspective.

Here are some Scriptures to study for faith to receive your healings and miracles.

- Exodus 23:25-26
- Deuteronomy 3:22
- Zechariah 3:17
- Psalm 84:11
- Psalm 86:15
- Psalm 91:9,10
- Psalm 103:2,3
- Psalm 107:20
- Proverb 4:20
- Isaiah 53:4
- Isaiah 54:17
- Isaiah 55:10
- Matthew 6:10
- Matthew 9:27-30
- Matthew 16:19
- Matthew 18:19
- Matthew 28:18
- Mark 9:23
- Mark 11:23,24
- Luke 10:19
- John 4:17,18
- John 14:12
- John 16:23
- John 20:29

- Romans 4:17-2
- Romans 8:11
- Romans 10:17
- Ephesians 3:20
- Philippians 2:9
- II Timothy 1:7
- Hebrews 6:12
- Hebrews 11:1
- Hebrews 11:6
- James 1:2-4,12
- James 4:7
- I John 3:8
- I John 4:4
- I John 5:14
- Revelation 12:11

PRAYERS FOR HEALING AND RESTORATION

I've always believed in the healing power of prayer as my mother was what some called a "prayer warrior" Whenever I and my siblings were ill my mother would rebuke the fever or whatever symptoms we were experiencing in the name of Jesus and declare us healed.

I truly experienced the healing power of prayer at a young age, and as a teenager I began researching natural solutions for illnesses. I have used natural medications from plants, herbs, vitamins and minerals and saw great results with prayer.

Given the correct natural substances and prayer, I firmly believe the human body can be healed and restored. Prayer is a very powerful medication. So is laughter!

Whatever your situation may be today, I pray these short prayers will bring you hope, healing and restoration as you are brought closer to your creator Yahweh, Jehovah Nissi (His banner over you is LOVE) and Jehovah Rapha, (the Lord who heals).

PRAYER FOR DIVINE HEALTH

Dear Heavenly Father,

I acknowledge you as the Creator God the one who spoke the worlds into existence. You created man as a perfect being; spirit, soul and body. Therefore, you desire that we prosper and be in good health as our soul prospers.

I ask you heavenly father please give me knowledge and wisdom to take the utmost care of my body to maintain good health.

I thank you heavenly father that I live in divine health in spite of being born into sin. I thank you for sending your son, Jesus, Yeshua so that through his pain and suffering (bleeding from the many stripes and flogging of his body) from the crucifixion I can experience divine health each and every day.

AMEN.

PRAYER FOR SOUL HEALING

Dear Jesus,

I'm coming to you because you died on the cross for my sins and you completed the task for my forgiveness, so that I may have eternal life with you in heaven one day.

Please forgive me of all my sins and become my Lord. I give my life to you. I desire to serve you . . . no longer just living for myself.

Thank you that you do forgive me and remove my sins as far as the east is from the west to the sea of forgetfulness. I'm no longer a slave to sin but now a child of God.

I choose to forgive those who have caused great harm to me and my family because you said if we don't forgive others, we won't be forgiven by God. I release my offenders to you in Jesus name. Now, please bring forth the healing of my soul. Pour out the healing balm upon my soul, which is your blood, Lord Jesus. In Jesus name I pray.

AMEN

PRAYER FOR HEALING FROM GRIEF

Dear Jesus,

I'm in the deep dark night of the soul, empty and devastated from my loss. You have borne our griefs and carried our sorrows. You have experienced what I'm feeling now at this moment.

Please bring your comfort and peace to me at this time. I need your soothing healing balm and your sweet smelling myrrh to touch me today. Please pour it out upon me now. I need your supernatural oil of gladness to overtake this spirit of heaviness that is upon me.

Thank you for sending your Holy Spirit as my comforter to comfort me during this time. I desire and look forward to the new day when my joy will be restored! Thank you, Jesus.

AMEN

PRAYER FOR HEALING OF ANXIETY

Dear Jesus,

You know my ways and see all that I am and all that I do. You know me well, so please allow me to feel your grace and love during his stressful time.

You see my emotional struggles and yearning to be free. So many times I have failed you and experience the cognitive dissonance in my life as a double minded person. My spirit is truly willing but my flesh is weak. The Apostle Paul said the things I need to do I don't do and the things I shouldn't be doing, that I do.

Draw me close to you so that during the times of stress I learn to lean on you and rest in you, instead of leaning on the arm of my flesh and human reasoning. Thank you for your mercy and grace. Help me to grow into becoming like you…into your image. Thank you, Jesus.

AMEN

PRAYER FOR HEALING FROM ADDICTIONS

Dear Jesus,

I know you want me to be whole and no longer broken so Lord please bind up my broken heart and set me on the path towards freedom. You said, "I am the way, the truth and the life!"

Jesus you died so I could be free! I accept your death as a finished work for myself. Therefore I resist the evil one – and reject disease and addictions controlling my life. Your word says whom the son has set free is free indeed.

Today I ask your Holy Spirit to come to me and break off of me every disease and addiction. Holy Spirit, you are so powerful! I desire to feel your Holy Spirit more than anything because it satisfies above all else.

AMEN

PRAYER FOR HEALING OF THE HEART

Dear Jesus,

Thank you for coming to heal the brokenhearted and set the captive free. As my heart is broken and torn so is my physical heart's condition, the same.

I ask you Jesus to bind up my broken heart and heal my physical heart as well. I declare my blood pressure is normal and its 120 over 80 and my heart is beating at an even pace, not erratic. I declare my arteries are clean and strong in the name of Jesus.

Help me to keep a heart healthy diet, one in which my heart can be properly nourished. I thank you for healing my body and my soul.

AMEN

PRAYER FOR PHYSICAL HEALING
OF INJURY

Dear Jesus,

I thank you that I am fearfully and wonderfully made! You created every part of my body in my mother's womb. You have woven together each part of my body perfectly.

Now I ask you to heal and restore my emotions from the trauma of this event and heal and restore my body to begin functioning as you created it to function.

Please mend the torn and broken parts of my body and may they speedily be restored in the name of Jesus Christ my Lord and Savior

Thank you, Jesus for taking the beating of 39 stripes on your back causing your blood to flow for my healing. I accept what you have done for my healing and I receive my healing and restoration now!

AMEN

Prayer for Physical Healing
of Disease

Dear God,

You said in your Word, the Bible, that you forgive, cleanse us from all our sins, and heal all our diseases. Holy Spirit, if this sickness and disease is due to sin and/or generational iniquity of my forefathers, please reveal it to me. (Wait in silence a few minutes to allow the Lord to reveal your sin or the sins of ancestors that have affected your DNA.)

God, you said iniquity (ancestral sins) follows the bloodline for several generations. Therefore, I pray that the sins of my ancestors be covered in Jesus' blood. I renounce all the sins of _____ and command that all DNA of _____sin in my bloodline and iniquity to leave my body now in the name of Jesus.

Thank you for removing this iniquity and declaring those sins covered by your precious blood, Lord Jesus.

AMEN

A GENERAL HEALING PRAYER

Dear Jesus,

When faith walks in, doubt, fear, anxiety, and unbelief walk out! Thank you, Jesus, that perfect love casts out fear. Our love isn't perfect, but your love for us is perfect. Therefore I use your name, Jesus, to rebuke this infirmity, infection and condition called,

_____

_____. (Fill in the blank.)

Thank you, Jesus, for the stripes you took for my healing. I receive my healing now in your name, Jesus. In your name, Jesus, I send every spirit of infirmity to the pit. My body is the temple of the Holy Spirit and belongs to you, Jesus. You have disarmed every power and principality and triumphed over them making a public spectacle out of them (Col. 2:15). Thank you, Jesus, for the victory!

AMEN.

I pray that after you pray these prayers, your situation will change by the power of the name of Jesus.

I want to add a note of caution here. This is not true in every case, but in some cases unforgiveness, anger, and bitterness can cause sickness and disease as well as prevent healing.

People can become addicted to OTC and prescription medications. I recommend the book *Pharmakia* by Ana Mendez Ferrell for more information about pharmaceuticals.

One does not need to pray these exact prayers to be healed. Each person should pray what he or she feels led to pray by the direction of the Holy Spirit. These are just examples to give you an idea as to how to pray. It is not a formula.

God heals in different ways, depending on how he wants to do it. Pray, expecting him to do it, and then always sit, waiting on God. Listen for any instructions he may bring to your spirit in a still small voice. Remember our faith is ONLY in God, and sometimes he tests our faith to see if we will go everywhere to solve the issue on our own or wait upon his direction and guidance. His way is the BEST! He loves it when we just trust him, as healing is HIS children's bread!

My prayer for you is 3 John 2 (NKJV).

Beloved, I pray that you may prosper in all things and be in health, just as your soul prospers.

OTHER BOOKS BY MK HENDERSON

Creating a Supernatural Lifestyle—
Angels and Miracles

Does God use angels to bring you miracles?
Find out in these true accounts of miracles.
(Also available as ebook on Amazon)

Supernatural Stories of Hope and Healing

True Inspirational Reports
from Around the World
(Also available as ebook on Amazon)

Healing and Restoring Children at Risk - $14.99

A manual for parents/caregivers of special needs children
(Also available as ebook on Amazon)

Sizzlers for Singles

53 Weeks of devotions with nuggets of wisdom
(Also available as ebook on Amazon)

*Survival Guide for Teens - $5.00 for series

A three part series of pocket gift books for
teens dealing with emotional pain.
All print books available on Amazon.

*Exception: A limited supply of the print books available
Email: readywriter@tutanota.com for an order form.

ENDNOTES

1. *New York Times,* 7 Nov. 2006
2. jglm.org/john-g-lake/
3. Lake, J., 2017. *Heavenly Authority: The Right Of The Believer.* p.29.
4. Kuhlman, Kathryn. "I Believe in Miracles and Healing in the Spirit." *Christianity Today*, 20 July 1973.
5. Wikipedia.org/wiki/Azusa_Street_Revival
6. Lake, J., 2017. *Heavenly Authority: The Right Of The Believer.* p.71.
7. Ibid, 87.

ABOUT THE AUTHOR

MK Henderson has a passion to see believers take that which God says is the "children's bread"—healing—even if they must fight the devil for it. She travels internationally as a healing ambassador to the nations. MK has earned bachelor degrees in Biblical Studies and Mass Communications with a sociology concentration from Evangel University. She also earned a master's degree in Television and Film Production from Regent University.

MK produces television programs of hope for women in third world countries in their own languages. Her love for people has led her to obey God. In sharing personal supernatural stories, it is her hope that they will stir up your appetite for more from God.